David Del Tredici
The Felix Variations

for Solo Bass Trombone

ISBN 978-1-4803-0874-9

BOOSEY & HAWKES

AN IMAGEM COMPANY

DISTRIBUTED BY

HAL•LEONARD®
CORPORATION
7777 W. BLUEMOUND RD. P.O. BOX 13819 MILWAUKEE, WI 53213

www.boosey.com
www.halleonard.com

Published by Boosey & Hawkes, Inc.
229 West 28th Street, 11th Fl
New York, NY 10001

www.boosey.com

 AN IMAGEM COMPANY

ISMN 979-0-051-10744-5

Engraving by Steven Burke and David Nadal
First printed 2012

Commissioned by, dedicated to, and inspired by my nephew, Felix Del Tredici

First performed on 12 April 2012 by Felix Del Tredici at
(Le) Poisson Rouge, New York, NY

COMPOSER'S NOTE

Commissioned by, dedicated to, and inspired by my nephew, Felix Del Tredici

Behind these dedicatory words lies a family story. I am the oldest of five – 4 boys and a girl. As well there are grandparents, aunts, uncles, cousins galore – but not one of these is in the least musical. That is, until my nephew Felix came along. Felix, at the tender age of 20, had developed into a virtuoso bass trombone player.

There is a family tradition: all of the East Coast brothers – David, Robert, Peter – gather for Christmas at Peter's house in Boston. In 2010, my brother Robert came and brought along his son Felix, trombone in hand. Robert had (of course) raved about Felix, but I had never heard him play. Well, play he did – so brilliantly, so unexpectedly musically and imaginatively that it took my breath away, and in that moment I decided to write him a piece. As I recall now, for 3 days after Christmas that year, a horrendous blizzard gripped the East Coast. Luckily, I had gotten back to New York City before it struck but I was then trapped in my apartment. In those three days I wrote my Felix piece: a set of variations on the famous theme of Paganini's 24th Caprice. Although this theme has for centuries inspired sets of variations from the greatest composers, I nevertheless decided to take it on.

The Felix Variations has (appropriately for a *Tredici*!) 13 variations, the last of which is longer – a *Finale*. That one could write for the bass trombone with almost violinistic agility confounded me – but I had just heard Felix do it. As well, he had shown me exotic trombone "effects" known to few, had demonstrated the wealth of muting possibilities, the drama of super low notes and the virtuosity of "impossible" high notes. All this I put into the *Variations* and for good measure a quote from my signature piece, *Final Alice*.

Felix premiered the piece (his NY debut) on April 12 of 2012 at (Le) Poisson Rouge in New York City. It was a celebration of my 75th birthday. I received no greater gift than that night's dazzling performance.

–*David Del Tredici*
August 16, 2012

Commissioned by, dedicated to, and inspired by my nephew, Felix Del Tredici

THE FELIX VARIATIONS
for solo bass trombone

DAVID DEL TREDICI
(2010)

979-0-051-10744-5

Var. 3
Allegro vivace (♩ = 144)

※ con "cup" sord.

※ Insert mute while sustaining the note.

Var. 4
Poco meno mosso (♩ = 120)

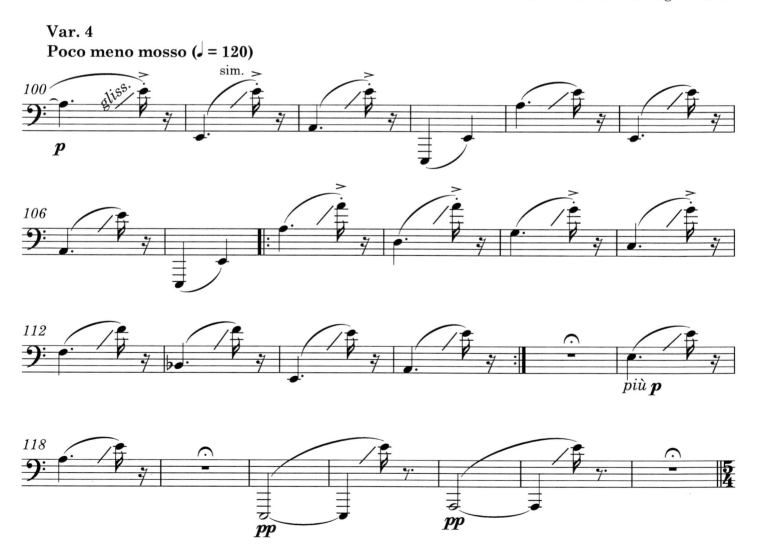

Var. 5: Romanza ✻
Adagio (♩ = 56)
senza sord., con vib.

mf cantabile e rubato

✻ *Acrostic Song* theme from the composer's 1976 work, FINAL ALICE.

Var. 6
Molto allegro (♩ = 138)
con Harmon sord. – stem out ✻

✻ Player must connect the Harmon mute to a stand to avoid a lengthy pause between the variations.

4

6

December 26–28, 2010
New York City